D0842901

EXPLORING AFRICAN CIVILIZATIONS™

DISCOVERING
THE ASANTE KINGDOM

ROBERT Z. COHEN

ROSEN PUBLISHING®

New York

Published in 2014 by The Rosen Publishing Group, Inc.
29 East 21st Street, New York, NY 10010

Library of Congress Cataloging-in-Publication Data

Cohen, Robert Z.
Discovering the Asante kingdom/Robert Z. Cohen.—First edition.
        pages cm.—(Exploring African civilizations)
Includes bibliographical references and index.
ISBN 978-1-4777-1880-3 (library binding)
1. Ashanti (Kingdom)—Juvenile literature. 2. Ashanti (African people—History—Juvenile literature. 3. Ashanti (African people)—Social life and customs—Juvenile literature. I. Title. II. Series: Exploring African civilizations.
DT507.C65 2014
966.7018—dc23

2013017406

Manufactured in the United States of America

CPSIA Compliance Information: Batch #W14YA: For further information, contact Rosen Publishing, New York, New York, at 1-800-237-9932.

A portion of the material in this book has been derived from *The Asante Kingdom* by Carol Thompson.

CONTENTS

INTRODUCTION

I n the late 1600s, the Asante kingdom—located in today's nation of Ghana and often written as "Ashanti"—rose to become the greatest empire on the west coast of Africa.

Asante was unique among the many kingdoms that faced the arrival of European colonial power in Africa. Inspired by a divine vision, Asante's first king, Osei Bonsu, developed a new type of political state. Asante rule was not based on the person of the king but on a set of moral and practical principles embodied in the symbol of the state: the Golden Stool.

The inspiration of the Golden Stool led the Asante kingdom to become very rich—in gold, in slaves, in guns, and in influence. A strong identity gave the Asante the confidence to overcome political rivalries that had weakened many of the small kingdoms of the West African coast. It also provided the sense of purpose that allowed the Asante to treat the encroaching European powers as equals. Asante rulers never felt inferior to Europeans, and when pushed to fight, the Asante became legendary for their dogged resistance to colonial domination.

No history of any part of West Africa can be told without acknowledging the important role of the four-hundred-year-old slave trade from Africa to the Americas. During the eighteenth century, nearly 700,000 people from the region of modern-day Ghana were enslaved and sent to the New World. At times, the Asante people were sold into slavery by their enemies. At other times, they sold their enemies to be shipped

Modern Asantes balance keeping their traditions alive with being proud Ghanaians in a changing Africa.

across the ocean. Slavery was a terrible and evil institution: its influence lingers through history to this day. The blood of the Asante and other Akan peoples flows through many of their descendants who live in North and South America today.

The Asante kingdom grew by persuading neighboring states to join the Asante Confederacy, a union of smaller states.

The core of the Asante Confederacy was made up of people who lived within a 20-mile (32 kilometers) radius of Kumasi, the capital of the Asante region. In the 1700s, at the height of its expansion, the Asante kingdom's influence extended beyond the borders of modern-day Ghana, making it the largest kingdom in West Africa at the time. For the British, who were asserting their military power to make the Gold Coast a British colony, the Asante were unlike any of the other peoples they had faced. The Asante resisted fiercely and stubbornly, never betraying their inspired vision of the Golden Stool and the unique fate that their first king, Asantehene Osei Bonsu, had set for them.

CHAPTER ONE

The Akan World

The Asante are but one of the many Akan peoples who live along the west coast of Africa in what is today Ghana and Cote d'Ivoire. The Akan are connected by a shared language—the version spoken by the Asante is called Twi—and many shared cultural traditions. Traditionally, Akan peoples organized themselves in small kingdoms, such as Bono Manso, Akwamu, Akyem, Fante, and Denkyira.

The various Akan groups have a history of rivalry between kingdoms. Before 1680, the Asante were under the domination of an Akan kingdom to their west, Denkyira, which had become the most powerful state in the region by 1650. Along the coast to the south, the Akan group known as the Fante controlled access to the valuable trade forts of the Europeans.

A Forest Full of Gold

The Asante region is covered in thick tropical forest. The Asante believe that they literally hacked a space for their culture— their cities, farms, and shrines—out of the dense forest. Stone axes—no longer needed since the introduction of modern

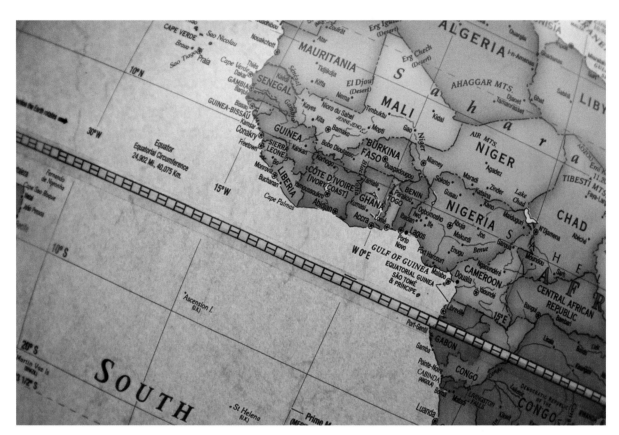

The geographic area of modern Ghana, where the Asante kingdom was located, was long known as the "Gold Coast." Most European traders visited only the coastal regions and never ventured inland to the source of the gold.

metal axes—are placed in shrines to the Supreme Creator Onyame in gratitude to their ancestors for their triumph over the forest.

The Akan lands, especially the central Asante region, have rich gold deposits and a long tradition of trading gold to the northern peoples of the Sahel, the dry grassland that borders the Sahara Desert. Scholars believe that the Akan peoples learned the skills of metalworking and weaving from people to the north in about the fourteenth century.

For many centuries before the founding of the Asante kingdom, gold had been mined in West Africa south of the Sahara

Desert. Gold was the basis of long-distance trade between Africans and the Muslim world, which used gold as currency. The Akan were drawn into this West African network of gold trading by the fourteenth century. They panned gold from the rivers in the region and sold gold dust and nuggets to African traders, who, in turn, sold it for export to Arab countries. Gold dust became the Asante currency. Early European traders were so impressed by the trade in gold that they named the coast of Ghana the "Gold Coast" (to the west was the "Ivory Coast" and to the east the "Slave Coast").

Earth and Spirit in Asante

In the Akan region, all land was organized into urban states, called *oman* in the Twi language. Each *oman* had its own ruler, or *omanhene*. He ruled over a hierarchy of chiefs, subchiefs, councils of elders, priests, artisans, and young men's groups.

Today, as in the past, the basis of Akan society is the family. Asante trace their descent through the blood of their mother, a practice known as matrilineal descent. Among the Asante, a person inherits according to the mother's family line, known as the *abasua*. This applies to the office of king as well. Unlike European systems in which the father confers royalty, Asante kings were named by a queen mother.

The Asante and other Akan peoples consider their ancestors vital and ever-present members of the family. The family does not consist only of the living. It is believed that the ancestors will protect the family if their living relatives pay them proper respect by remembering and honoring them. The worlds of the living and the dead are thus closely connected.

Seats of Power

Wooden stools are a sacred symbol of status and power and perhaps are the most important objects in Asante daily life. The Asante believe that a person's soul resides in his or her stool. The stool is therefore a very personal object, generally used only by its owner. It is turned on its side when not being used as a seat so that the souls of passing ancestors may not rest on it.

When an important person dies, such as an elder, priest, chief, military officer, or queen mother, his or her stool is

More than mere chairs, Asante stools could symbolize the power of a person's soul—or even a nation's destiny.

blackened with ashes. It is then placed in a special stool room along with those of other important members of the community. An Asante stool appears on the official flag of the Asante kingdom.

Osei Tutu: The Vision of a Kingdom

When Osei Tutu was born in 1660, the Asante *oman*, or state, was made up of seven chiefdoms, which were loosely allied but were also rivals. The entire Asante state was ruled by the powerful state of Denkyira to the south. Denkyira and the nearby Fante state controlled trade with the Europeans along the Atlantic coast. Denkyira had attacked the Asante with weapons obtained from the Europeans. The Asante were forced to pay tribute—in gold and in slaves—to Denkyira.

When Osei Tutu was young, the leader of the small Asante state was his great-uncle, Obiri Yeboa. Obiri Yeboa sent the young prince Osei Tutu to the court of Boa Amponsem, the ruler of Denkyira. There, Osei Tutu studied Akan law and customs and learned diplomacy. The event that most influenced his future, however, was meeting the influential priest Okomfo Anokye, who became his closest friend.

When Obiri Yeboa died, Osei Tutu returned to Kumasi with Okomfo Anokye as his companion and adviser. They decided to call the seven chiefdoms of the Asante people to a great meeting. It would take place under the sacred *kuma* tree that stood at the center of Kumasi's market and for which the city had been named. Messengers spread news throughout the region that each of the seven chiefs was to bring his sacred stool to the meeting, held on a Friday, and that Okomfo Anokye

WHAT'S IN A NAME?

The Akan peoples, including the Asante, attach much importance to names. Children are named after the day of the week on which they are born, as well as the order in which they are born in relationship to siblings. They also receive a name identifying them as being of a certain place and family. All male children born on a Saturday are named Kwame, for example, while all Saturday-born girls are named Amma.

This practice spread to other peoples along the West African coast as well, and slaves taken from this region brought it with them to the New World. Many Akan descendants kept the naming tradition but adapted it to the English language. Among the last families to maintain the Akan names in the United States were free black families who had intermarried with New England Native American communities. Paul Cuffee (1759–1815) was half Asante and half Wampanoag Indian. His name comes from *Kofi*, or "Friday-born." He became a rich sea captain and antislavery activist. He worked to make Sierra Leone a haven for Africans who wished to return to Africa. Wickham Cuffee was an influential leader of New York's Shinnecock Indians. Some of his descendants are famous today as members of the hip-hop supergroup Wu-Tang Clan.

Day of the Week	Male Name	Female Name
Monday	Kwadwo / Kojo	Adowa
Tuesday	Kwabena	Abenaa
Wednesday	Kwaku	Akua
Thursday	Yaw	Yaa
Friday	Kofi	Afia
Saturday	Kwame	Amma
Sunday	Akwasi	Akosua

would appoint a new ruler of all the Asante. When the chiefs gathered, they placed their stools in the center of the meeting place. Okomfo Anokye began to dance and entered into a trance, during which he communicated with Nyankopon, the Supreme Being.

According to Asante lore, Nyankopon sent a bolt of lightning that consumed the seven stools of the Asante chiefs, covering the area with a dark cloud of smoke. When the smoke cleared, a blackened stool descended from the sky to rest on the knees of Osei Tutu. As the crowd watched, the blackened stool turned to gold.

Okomfo Anokye announced that Nyankopon had clearly shown through these magical events that the seven Asante groups should cease their conflicts and be united as one nation ruled by Osei Tutu. The *Sika Dwa Kofi*, the "Golden Stool created on Friday," became the symbol of the new nation. Just as the stools of living people and the dead were the resting places

The Golden Stool represents the entire history and fate of the Asante people and is always treated with utter respect.

for their souls, the Golden Stool contained the *sumsum*, or soul, of the Asante nation. The Golden Stool was far more spiritually powerful than any other stool. Nobody—not even the king—would ever sit on it because nobody had the right to oppress the Asante nation or regard himself or herself as superior to it.

These events, which occurred sometime in the 1670s, gave the Asante a new unity. The seven chiefs all swore loyalty to Osei Tutu, who took the title *Asantehene*—King of the Asante.

The people of the kingdom were urged to forget previous rivalries and place their loyalties with the Golden Stool. Allegiance to it guaranteed their wealth and welfare. So long as the Asante peoples acted as allies, the safety and prosperity of the kingdom were assured.

Osei Tutu received tribute and military support from each of the chiefs and created new laws that applied to everyone in the Asante kingdom. He allowed each of his allied kingdoms to retain their own king and court, which would send representatives to the Asantehene in Kumasi. The new Asante kingdom was now a direct threat to Denkyira.

CHAPTER TWO

A New Power Rises

Asante's first king, Osei Tutu, was a talented ruler who created new strategies to unify and expand the young kingdom. He created a new constitution, declared the town of Kumasi the kingdom's capital, and established an annual state celebration in Kumasi called the *Odwira* festival, which all members of the Asante Confederacy were required to attend. The festival encouraged a sense of peace and unity within the kingdom.

Osei Tutu then turned to reforming the Asante army. The principle of the Golden Stool meant that a standing army was not needed: all able-bodied men would defend Asante when called. A unique defense strategy ensured that enemies would never be able to threaten the royal town of Kumasi. Tired of paying tribute to the kingdom of Denkyira, which had for so long oppressed the Asante and sold many into slavery, Asante allied itself with other tributaries. It finally threw off Denkyira rule at the Battle of Feyiase in 1701. The defeat of Denkyira opened up the last barrier to direct European trade along the Atlantic coast, at the Dutch-controlled fort of Elmina.

Osei Tutu continued to expand Asante territory. During the war against the Akan state of Akyem in 1717, a sniper shot

Osei Tutu while he was canoeing across the Pra River. Since that day, no Asante king has been allowed to travel farther south than the Pra River.

The empire that Osei Tutu had begun survived the loss of its charismatic first king. Osei Tutu's nephew, Opoku Ware, succeeded him and ruled as Asantehene until his death in 1750. A talented military leader, Opoku Ware transformed the Asante kingdom into the greatest power in the Akan region. He defeated the Akan states of Tekyiman in 1722–23 and Akyem in 1742, and he received tribute from other groups not fully incorporated into the Asante Confederacy. The influence of the kingdom extended well beyond the borders of modern-day Ghana.

Throughout this period of expansion, new villages and towns sprang up quickly. Like spokes of a wheel, roads radiated outward from Kumasi to all areas of Asante control and influence. These were vital for long-distance trade and the travel of royal officials and messengers.

The Role of Slavery

The Portuguese had been the first Europeans to sail to West Africa and trade along the coast. In 1482, the local Akan chiefs granted them permission to build the fort of Elmina, which means "the mine," on the coast, where its ruins still stand today. At first the Portuguese traded metals—particularly brass and copper—for gold, ivory, and other African goods. They were delighted to have established direct contact with the gold-producing areas of West Africa. Up to that time,

Built in 1482 by the Portuguese, Elmina Castle became one of the slave-trading posts that dotted the coast of West Africa. It is maintained as a museum and monument today.

Europe had been obliged to obtain most of its gold from Muslim traders who had carried the African gold north across the Sahara Desert.

Sugarcane and Slavery

Before Christopher Columbus encountered the Americas in 1492, sugar was one of the most rare and valuable commodities known to Europe. The most common sweetener before

1500 was honey made by bees. Sugar was considered an expensive spice.

Sugarcane could grow in only warm and wet climates, and it was produced mostly on plantations on the Mediterranean islands of Cyprus and Sicily. The plantations were worked mainly by Slavs from the Ukraine (their name was the origin of the word "slave"), who were captured and sold at Genoese ports around the Black Sea. After the fall of Constantinople to the Ottoman Turks in 1454, this source of slaves was cut off to Europe. The Portuguese began to use African slaves for their sugar plantations in Sao Tomé and Cabo Verde, islands off the coast of Africa. After Europeans explored the Americas, Native Americans were enslaved to work on sugarcane plantations, but they were no match for the imported diseases of the Old World and were soon replaced by Africans. In 1532, enslaved Africans were first transported across the Atlantic to the Americas, where the Portuguese and Spanish had established sugar plantations and mines.

Gradually Africa became more important to Portugal and other European nations as a source of slaves and products such as ivory, rather than gold. Enslaved Africans were taken from several parts of the West African coast, from present-day Senegal in the west to the Congo and Angola in the south. The Guinea coast, in the region of what is now Ghana, was an important center for this terrible trade in enslaved people.

Dutch Partners

By the time of the rise of Osei Tutu and Opoku Ware, the power of the Portuguese on the coast had declined. The

THE FIRST ASANTE DIASPORAS

Before the defeat of Denkyira, and even afterward, many Asante were sold into slavery in the New World. They were noted for their resistance to slavery and advanced levels of organization. Many ran away to freedom in the wilderness, forming communities of free slaves who raided the sugar plantations and defended their freedom. These communities were called Maroons, from the Spanish word *cimarrón*, which means "runaway" or "fugitive." The Akan language they spoke was known as Kromanti, since the slaves had often been shipped through Fort Koromantyn on the Gold Coast.

Many of the historical figures that led slave revolts in America can be traced to the Akan people through their names. The New York City Slave Revolt of 1712 was led by two slaves with Akan names: Cuffee (Kofi) and Quaco (Kwaku). Denmark Vesey, leader of the 1822 slave rebellion in South Carolina, was an Asante descendant born in the British Virgin Islands, where many Asante had been sold into slavery. Kromanti slaves were considered so dangerous that the Colony of Virginia tried to ban the import of more slaves from the region of Fort Koromantyn.

In Jamaica, Maroons hid out in the steep "cockpit" hill country and raided the lowlands, looting and freeing slaves. Led by leaders Cudjoe and Queen Nanny—both Akan names—the Trelawney Maroons fought the British until 1795. Those who refused to sign a treaty were rounded up and sent to Nova Scotia, Canada, but the cold winters proved fatal to them. Many were then sent to Sierra Leone in Africa, where they formed the beginnings of a new "Krio" (creole) society.

Today, there are still Maroon communities in Jamaica, often in towns with Akan names, such as Accompong and Cudjoe Town. Maroons in Guyana and Suriname fled into the jungle and developed a version of Akan culture and religion that exists today among the peoples known as Ndjuka, Saramaka, and Kwinti.

Dutch took over Elmina Castle. The British established a fort at Cape Coast in a region controlled by the Fante, bitter rivals of the Asante.

By the time Opoku Ware died in 1750, the Asante kingdom controlled all of the region's major trade routes from the interior to the sea. Opoku Ware had even negotiated a treaty to collect rent from the new Dutch owners of Elmina Castle, the most important European trading fort in all of West Africa.

The Dutch regarded the Asante as their main African trading partners. Two interesting examples illustrate the relationship between the Netherlands and the Asante kingdom: Asantehene Opoku Ware ordered a coffin from Holland, and in 1826, the Asante presented the Dutch with a special Asante cloth that had the Dutch coat of arms printed in the center.

Growth in the Grasslands

Through trade with the Dutch and other Europeans, the Asante obtained the firearms needed to challenge rival kingdoms. The Asante also used slaves to mine gold in order to meet the Europeans' demand for the precious metal. Within Asante society, however, slaves were considered a class of people with certain rights, not objects that were bought and owned. Slaves worked in mines as well as produced food on farms. Almost one-third of the population of Asante had slave status.

Asante gold mines were traditionally small pit mines, but modern mining methods cause major concern for the environment.

Blocked from expanding their influence to the south by the British-backed Fante Confederacy, Asante focused its expansion toward the grasslands of the north. In 1744–45, Asante soldiers with firearms easily defeated the cavalry of Dagomba, a northern state in whose open country the Asante had never before been prepared to fight. The Asante held Dagomba as a tributary state for nearly one hundred years. By the mid-eighteenth century, the Asante had also taken control of the cotton-producing city of Salaga, inhabited by the neighboring Gonja people.

Reforms and Rivals: Osei Kwadwo

Osei Kwadwo inherited the position of Asantehene after the death of Opoku Ware, reigning from 1764 to 1777. He introduced changes that increased the authority of the central government in Kumasi and professionalized the king's civil service. Bureaucrats were appointed according to their abilities, rather than their family ties.

Osei Kwadwo paid special attention to the administration of trade. He appointed officials to control trade from Kumasi and created a treasury to run the finances of the kingdom. Many of the treasury staff were Muslims from the grassland kingdoms north of Asante. Their skills in mathematics and Arabic writing were of particular use to the Asantehene, since the Asante did not then have a tradition of writing.

During Osei Kwadwo's reign, tension increased between the Asante and the Fante to the south, and in 1765, they fought. From that time onward, they would continue to have periodic conflicts, even after Osei Kwadwo's death.

CHAPTER THREE

A State of Beauty: Asante Art

A public display of wealth—in gold, fine cloth, and imported European luxury goods—was considered an important statement of status and power for people who followed the Asante way of life. The king's wealth was a reflection of Asante power, and the Asantehene's palace in Kumasi was the showpiece of Asante art and wealth. Any Asante subject could visit the royal palace and be fed at any time. It was a living symbol of the unifying power of the Golden Stool.

Gold was a major source of the Asante kingdom's wealth, and the Asantehene controlled its use, sale, and taxation. Gold was seen as an earthly counterpart to the sun and the physical manifestation of life's vital force, or *kra* ("soul"). The metal was incorporated into the ruler's regalia to represent his purity and vigor, as well as indicate his kingdom's dominance over rivals. Gold was on display in the court, where the royal family and important officials wore special items of dress given to them by the king. These included gold jewelry and gold leaf–covered swords, staffs, headdresses, tunics, sandals, and other items.

Regalia

Some items of regalia were reserved for certain types of officials. Sword-bearers, for example, served as the king's ambassadors, messengers, and escorts for visitors to the kingdom. The counselors and spokesmen of Akan chiefs still carry staffs topped with gold-covered sculptures that refer to well-known Akan proverbs. A sculpture of a man holding an egg, for example, refers to the proverb that power is like an egg: if it is not held carefully, it can easily fall from one's grasp, and if held too tightly, it will be crushed.

The Great Chest of Gold

The Asante gold reserve was called the *Adaka Kese*, or Great Chest. Nearly 7 feet (2.1 meters) long and 4 feet (1.2 meters) wide, it contained about 25,000 pounds (11,340 kilograms) of gold dust and nuggets, worth about $160 million today. The *gyaasewahene*, or head of the king's civil service, was the guardian of the Great Chest and held the only key to the room where it was kept.

The Asantehene, however, could afford to be lavish with gold dust. Visitors to the kingdom in the eighteenth century described how Asantehene Opoku Ware's servants oiled the king's skin and hair and powdered him completely with fine gold dust twice a day. Only then was he ready to appear in public.

The king controlled the goldsmiths of Kumasi. Senior chiefs had to obtain the permission of the Asantehene before they

WEAVING WEALTH: KENTE CLOTH

The brightly colored striped cloth known as kente is probably the most widespread and famous of Asante arts. To create kente, complex patterns are woven into narrow strips, which are then sewn together to form a large piece of cloth. The intricate skill involved in weaving kente led Akan people to link it to the stories of the mythological spider, Anansi. One story tells how Anansi the spider used his web to teach two brothers to dye and weave kente cloth. As in the story, kente is typically woven by men.

Kente announces the wearer's status and wealth. Traditionally, the very best are reserved for the Asantehene and other important leaders. When Europeans brought cloth into the kingdom in the 1700s, the Asantehene ordered the finest fabrics, including Chinese silks, to be unraveled and rewoven into Asante-style cloth for his personal use.

Like many African arts, the patterns of the cloth serve as more than simple decoration: they can embody ideas reflecting history, philosophy, religion, and politics. Each pattern has a particular name. Kente colors carry meanings. An informed person can "read" a kente cloth like a book.

Kente has become part of many modern African fashion designs and has been widely adopted by many African Americans as a symbol of pride in their African roots. While genuine handwoven kente is expensive, bright kente patterns are printed onto cheaper fabrics and incorporated into T-shirts, scarves, and even baseball hats.

Intricately woven kente cloth announces the status of its wearer. Kente has become popular across Africa and beyond.

could commission gold ornaments from these highly skilled craftsmen. A 1909 colonial survey showed that eighty-five goldsmiths worked in or near Kumasi. They accompanied Asante armies into battle in order to make the portrait sculptures of slain enemies. These portraits were used to adorn Asante stools and swords.

Brass counterweights for weighing gold are a distinctive Asante art form. Many are in the form of people, plants, animals, or scenes of daily life. Often these images relate to proverbs. A weight showing a leopard with a gun in its mouth

In Asante culture, the brass counterweights used to measure raw gold were themselves works of art.

standing over a hunter, for example, refers to the proverb, "Think before you act."

Shaded Pleasure

The Asante associated shade with power. Every chief was expected to plant a new shade tree when he took power, decorate the shade trees of his predecessors with white cloth, and vow to rule well and guard his people. Before going to war, a chief vowed to his people that their enemy would not be

Shade and breezes, provided by umbrellas, were considered luxuries to be exhibited by the Asante royalty during public celebrations.

allowed to enter the city and cut down the tree he had planted. After each war, new trees were planted. When a chief died, it was said, "A great tree has fallen." Trees like the sacred *kuma* of Kumasi were regarded as signs of a city's physical and spiritual well-being.

Umbrellas play a similar role in Asante culture. Any Asante festival or procession moves beneath the billowing, pulsating cover of numerous huge umbrellas. Traditionally, Asante chiefs appeared in public under huge umbrellas that were associated with shade trees. They were said to provide both physical coolness and spiritual coolness, or calm. They are still used on state occasions. While moving along, the umbrellas are lifted up and down, providing a cooling breeze along with the shade.

CHAPTER FOUR

Clash of Empires

Asante power and prosperity reached their peak during the reign of Asantehene Osei Bonsu between 1779 and 1824. Gold and slaves were traded for guns, iron, and luxury goods through the Dutch and Danish trading forts on the coast. English goods—particularly their superior firearms—were obtained via Fante middleman traders. In 1805, the Asante attacked the British fort at Abora, where several Fante soldiers had taken refuge. The Asante defeated the Fante and were acknowledged as the rulers of the coast.

In 1806, however, the Fante killed an Asante diplomatic envoy accompanied by a sword-bearer and seized the royal golden sword. The incident outraged the Asante, who marched south to invade the Fante region in 1807. After a long conflict, the Asante eventually retreated, while the Fante grew more dependent on the British for arms and protection.

By the late eighteenth century, calls for the abolition of the slave trade influenced several European powers to suspend their African coastal slave trade. Important religious thinkers, influenced by the Quaker religion, pointed out the evils of slave ownership in widely distributed writings and sermons. In 1807, the British outlawed slavery, as the Danes had done five years earlier. The Spanish and Portuguese, however, continued to buy slaves for export to the sugar plantations of Cuba and Brazil. The fight against the coastal slave trade reduced one of the most profitable trading activities of the Asante and one of the cornerstones of their relationship with Europeans.

Increasing Contact with Europeans

Gradually, the Asante came into closer contact with the Europeans. For their own use, Asante leaders imported such goods as cloth, liquor, silver vessels, clothing, flags, gold-topped canes, elaborate hats, carriages, magic lanterns, lathes, and leather shoes.

Another sign of the kingdom's increased openness was the number of foreigners employed by the Asantehene during Osei Bonsu's reign. For the first time, Europeans were allowed in the civil service as a way to secure more European trade items. Trading agents, such as Englishman Thomas Edward Bowdich, described Kumasi as an orderly, clean, and comfortable city of about forty thousand residents. To ensure the safety of the confederacy and guard against revolts by lesser chiefs, the Asantehene had a special security force in Kumasi called the *Ankobia*, which functioned as a secret police force.

Asante military power—fed by the regular exchange of gold for guns with the Dutch at Elmina—kept the British and their Fante allies in a state of constant alert. Although the Asante had conquered them, the Fante protected their access to British trade and were never fully absorbed into the Asante Confederacy. They retained their independence, and their armies were never disbanded.

Osei Bonsu the Builder

To celebrate his victories, Osei Bonsu initiated many building projects to improve the capital city and its roads. Army captains returning from war were rewarded with large sums of gold from the royal treasury to decorate or enlarge their houses.

For himself, Osei Bonsu erected the great Stone Palace, modeled after the Europeans' coastal forts. The building, decorated with gold, ivory, and brass, was completed in 1822. It was mainly used as a treasure storehouse, especially for precious items from overseas. Pots of food were always available to any Asante citizen who arrived hungry. Storerooms held the Asantehene's finery, the royal *atumpan* drums, and stocks of imported European brandy and champagne. On the upper floors of the Stone Palace were the art treasures of the monarchy, including the Asantehene's collection of books in various languages, paintings, engravings, carpets, glass, silver, clocks, and fine furniture.

Two Empires Clash

During the second half of the nineteenth century, the Asante struggled to balance opposing social and political forces. The demand for profit and power made them reliant on war and conquest, yet successful trade demanded peace. The acquisition of personal wealth led to political corruption. Asantehene Kwaku Dua, who ruled from 1834 to 1867, replaced advisers with personal cronies and business partners. This exploitation of the position would eventually weaken the office of Asantehene just as the British threat loomed largest.

TALKING DRUMS

The Asante communicated over large areas of their forested empire by using "talking drums." Each palace held a set of royal drums that could be heard over great distances. Drummers would then relay messages to the next town.

These drummed messages were not simply signals but reproductions of spoken language. Most West African languages are "tone languages" (as are Chinese, Thai, and Navaho) that use word pitch to transmit meaning. The Twi word *papa*, for example, can mean "father," "fan," or "good," depending on its tonal melody. Drummers can vary the pitch of their drums using different strokes and approximate the sounds of some vowels and consonants. Typically, drummers repeat phrases or embed them in a kind of poetry.

West African drummers often drum texts praising important or rich people, who then pay them in tips. In many traditions, the voice of the drum is considered to come directly from the world of the ancestors. Drummers are thus allowed to make sly or critical statements without any fear of personal reprisal. In one Asante town, the king was carried in a palanquin on his court's shoulders in a festival procession. Large royal drums announced the king's importance in drum language to the crowd: "The king is heavy! The king is heavy!" Along the parade route, common people with smaller drums played an accompanying rhythm that taunted, "Cut him up and make him smaller!"

Asante and other Akan people sold as slaves to the New World brought their musical traditions with them. The oldest collected object from African American history, an Akan drum collected around 1730 in Virginia, is on display at the British Museum in London. Made from wood found only in Africa but using a deerskin drumhead from America, it resembles the royal *atumpan* drums of the Asante. Slaves fighting for their freedom used talking drums to communicate during the Stono Slave Rebellion of 1739 in South Carolina. Afterward, all African drums were banned in the North American colonies as dangerous weapons.

Drums are not just for dancing. Messages and announcements are communicated in the beats played by expert drum masters.

In 1849, Britain declared the entire Gold Coast to be a British protectorate and assured several of the Fante kingdoms that if attacked, Britain would help defend them. Friction between the governments soon arose when runaway slaves, corrupt officials, or tax debtors fled from Asante territory south into the protectorate to escape punishment.

When the Dutch finally left their trading settlements and Fort Elmina to the British in 1869, Asantehene Kofi Kakari, who ruled from 1867 to 1874, was outraged. The Dutch had taken control of the old Portuguese fort when the kingdom of Denkyira was in power. The Asante had defeated Denkyira and thus, in the Asantehene's view, the Dutch had no right to give the English what was rightfully theirs. When the English occupying the fort refused to pay taxes to the Asante, Kofi Kakari demanded that the protectorate kingdoms of Denkyira, Assin, and Akim be returned to him. By 1873, war with the British was unavoidable.

Facing the Asante, the British tried a new military strategy. Instead of sending more British troops, they provided thousands of modern breech-loading guns to the Fante and their other Akan allies in the protectorate to use against the Asante. Having proclaimed their authority over part of the coastal region, the British began to push the Asante inland and pressed on toward the Asante capital at Kumasi. When the Asantehene and his court fled Kumasi, British forces led by Field Marshal Garnet Wolseley entered the city and burned part of it. They looted and dynamited the Stone Palace. They cut down Kumasi's sacred *kuma* tree. Furthermore, the British demanded that the Asante pay an astonishing 50,000 troy ounces

During the Asante War, the British used local troops recruited from neighboring rival Akan peoples to attack Asante towns.

(1,555,174 grams) of gold to cover the cost of the British military expedition; accept the presence of a British official to be stationed in Kumasi; and, most shocking to the Asante, surrender the Golden Stool. The Asante accepted peace but refused to surrender the revered Golden Stool.

The defeat by the British was blamed on the ruling Asantehene's ambitious schemes to raise taxes and use money from the special "Stool Treasury," which had made him unpopular. The council of elders, the *mpanyimfo*, met and voted to "de-stool" the king on October 26, 1874. According to their judgment, Kofi Kakari had failed to live up to the office of Asantahene and was not worthy of the power of the Golden Stool. His brother, Mensa Bonsu, succeeded him and promised a policy of peace and trade. Instead, Mensa Bonsu continued the unpopular practice of taxing and spending from the Stool Treasury. He built a standing army comprised of the Muslim Hausa tribe from the north. Now protected by the British military, more and more local chiefs withdrew their loyalty from the Asante Confederacy in Kumasi. For the first time in its history, the kingdom of Asante grew weak.

CHAPTER FIVE

The Golden Stool in Decline

The last decades of the nineteenth century were a very difficult time for the people of the Asante kingdom. After the War of 1874, the kingdom was unwillingly declared a British Protectorate. British companies began mining gold in Adanse and the southern Asante region.

The appointment of Mensa Bonsu as Asantehene did not bring peace to the Asante. The new king continued the same corrupt policies of favoritism and increased taxation that had made his predecessor so unpopular. Under British protection, outlying states began to break away from the central control of Kumasi. Mensa Bonsu forced chiefs that he suspected of disloyalty to pay heavy fines in gold, often stripping them of all the wealth that symbolized their status as Asante minor kings. By the 1880s, the Asante treasury was nearly bankrupt.

Unhappy with the new Asantehene, a traditional priest claiming to be the reincarnation of Okomfo Anokye (the priest who founded the Asante kingdom with Osei Bonsu) attempted to assassinate Mensa Bonsu in 1880. The coup plot failed, but by 1883, the situation had erupted into a civil war. The enraged Mensa Bonsu retreated into the Asantehene's palace in Kumasi and placed kegs of gunpowder all around it, threatening to

Field Marshal Wolseley's victory in the 1874 Asante War was welcomed by Asante rivals such as the Fante of Cape Coast. But the Asante would soon face more serious challenges—internal dissent and civil war.

blow himself and the palace to smithereens if the revolt did not end. His brother, the dethroned ex-king Kofi Kakari, led an army into Kumasi and captured the palace.

The noble stool holders of the elder's council, however, did not wish to see either of the brothers as the new Asantehene. While the elders debated a course of action, ragged armies rampaged outside Kumasi, looting farms and towns. The carefully maintained road systems soon reverted to jungle paths. Kumasi was nearly deserted, and starvation threatened. A new Asantehene, Kwaku Dua II, died of illness soon after taking office, and Asante was without a king for some years after.

In 1889, a grandson of Kwaku Dua named Agyeman Prempeh was declared the best choice for the new Asantehene. Fighting ceased, and the British again offered to place the Asante region under direct protection. Agyeman Prempeh politely refused, declaring that Asante must remain independent and that state-controlled trade was once again running smoothly. The British again demanded a payment of 50,000 troy ounces (1,555,174 grams) of gold to pay for the costs of their military actions in Asante. Prempeh sent an Asante diplomatic delegation to meet with Queen Victoria, but they were refused an audience.

In January 1896, while Agyeman Prempeh negotiated with the British, Sir William Maxwell, governor of the Gold Coast Colony, sent troops to occupy Kumasi. They placed the Asantehene under arrest along with the members of his family. The Asantehene was exiled, first to Sierra Leone and then to the Seychelles Islands in the Indian Ocean. Prempeh, along with fifty-four family members, would return to Asante only in 1921.

BRITISH INDIRECT RULE

The British style of colonial rule was quite different from that practiced by other European colonial powers. While areas under French or German control were ruled directly by nonnative officials sent from Europe, the British developed a system called "indirect rule." The British sought to allow traditional rulers to retain their authority and political systems. The British colonial officials in charge took a hands-off approach to local matters and instead controlled external matters, taxes, and military functions. Developed first by the British governor of Nigeria, Frederick Lugard, indirect rule replaced heavy-handed, direct colonial rule in the Gold Coast Colony by the 1920s. This reduced the danger of revolts and allowed the British to influence local people through education in the missionary school systems.

Indirect rule also saved British lives. The tropical regions of West Africa had long been called the "white man's graveyard" due to the prevalence of malaria and other diseases. Before 1900, as many as one-third of all Europeans living on the coast of West Africa died of disease within a few years of arrival. Rather than send a large number of administrators from England, the British preferred to groom a class of native civil servants educated in the British way of thinking.

Fante people from the coast were often recruited for military duties, as were Muslim Hausa people from the north. Officers were often recruited from among freed Jamaican Maroons who had been resettled in Sierra Leone, or members of the West Indian regiments from the British Caribbean. Many of these soldiers and policemen remained in Africa after their terms were up, marrying local women and assimilating into the new Gold Coast middle class. Because of this, English surnames are very common, especially among the Fante people in southern Ghana.

Yaa Asantewaa

With the Asantehene in exile, there was no one to assume leadership of Asante. On March 25, 1900, the new governor of the Gold Coast, Sir Frederick Hodgson, paid his first official visit to Kumasi. The governor again demanded that the costs for the 1874 war be paid to the British in full. Then, in a shocking surprise move, the governor demanded that the Golden Stool be brought to him to sit on.

The gathered Asante were outraged at the arrogance and ignorance of the demand. The Golden Stool was not simply a royal throne like those used in Europe. The *Sika Diwa Kofi* housed the collective soul—the *sumsum*—of the entire Asante people. In the evening, the chiefs held a secret meeting. According to an article in Lehman College's *Women's Studies Review*, Yaa Asantewaa, the Queen Mother of Ejisu-Juaben, arose and addressed the gathering:

No white man could have dared to speak to chief of the Asante in the way the Governor spoke to you chiefs this morning. Is it true that the bravery of the Asante is no more? I cannot believe it. It cannot be! I must say this: if you the men of Asante will not go forward, then we will. We, the women, will. I shall call upon my fellow women. We will fight the white men. We will fight till the last of us falls in the battlefields.

For the first time in Asante history, the elders' council chose a woman to be *sahene*, the leader of the army. Meanwhile, Hodgson had sent out troops to search for the Golden Stool.

The defiant patriotism of Yaa Asantewaa continues to inspire modern women across Africa.

The search was unsuccessful, and the stool remained hidden. Yaa Asantewaa unleashed a guerilla war against the British, harassing them along the roads and sniping at them in the forests until they could no longer leave their fort in Kumasi. Hodgson tried desperately to telegraph for reinforcements—until the Asante cut the wire. By April 25, Kumasi was surrounded by Asante armies. The governor, other British officials, and their African allies and captives were trapped in the British fort, short of food and ammunition.

After two months, the governor and some officers made a desperate escape to Cape Coast, leaving just 153 men defending the fort. The Asante made only small attacks on them. In the meantime, the British rushed 1,400 troops from other parts of Africa to suppress the Asante. After a three-month campaign, the British—now armed with repeating rifles and machine guns—defeated the Asante. Queen Yaa Asantewaa held out to the very end. She was finally captured in 1900 and sent to the Seychelles Islands to join Prempeh and the other Asante royals in exile. She died in 1921.

After the war that Yaa Asantewaa inspired, the British treated the Asante with far greater respect. To this day, the Asante still sing of the great woman leader who restored Asante pride: *"Yaa Asantewaa! Oba basia! Ogyina apremo ano! Waye be egyae!"* ("Yaa Asantewaa, the warrior woman who faces the cannon in battle, you have accomplished great things!")

CHAPTER SIX

The Asante Legacy

With the Asantehene's family and the charismatic leader Yaa Asantewaa in exile, and the Golden Stool secretly hidden, the British placed Kumasi and the Asante lands under full control of the Gold Coast Colony, creating the Asante Protectorate in 1902. Asante would no longer be a military threat to British rule in West Africa.

After the British defeated the Asante in 1900, the Golden Stool was secretly buried. It stayed hidden away until 1921, when it was found buried in a forest by road workers, who stole some of the gold ornaments from it. They were captured and sentenced to death, but the British intervened and sent the criminals into exile far away from the country.

A King Returns

In 1924, the British released Prempeh I from his island exile. He agreed to rule as king of the Asante but to recognize the authority of the British over the Gold Coast. The British, still wary of a resurgence of the Asante Confederacy, allowed Prempeh I to adopt the title of *Kumasahene*, or King of Kumasi.

In 1933, the Asante Confederacy was restored. Two years later, in 1935, Prempeh II was enthroned as Asantehene, and the Golden Stool was displayed in public for the first time since 1896. To many, this demonstrated that the Asante had, throughout this period of resistance, preserved their soul, their *sumsum*.

The Birth of Ghana

During his long exile, Prempeh II learned English to prepare for a new leadership role in the modern era.

With peace restored, Kumasi and the Asante region again prospered. Schools were built, and many were run by European missionary societies. Many Asante became Christians while still maintaining many of their traditional religious beliefs.

Many Asante began to sense a connection with other groups of people living under the colonial rule of Britain. They used their western education to advocate for the idea of a new and independent African state. In 1957, Ghana became the first African state to become independent of European colonial rule. While the many regions and ethnic groups of the new state remained distinct, its citizens now proudly proclaimed a new identity: no longer subjects of the British queen, they were citizens of Ghana. Ghana remained a member of the British Commonwealth, an association of nations with close ties to Britain in trade and administration. Soon Ghanaians were going abroad for jobs, education, and forming clubs and societies to maintain their identity. The Asante maintain many such associations in Britain, the United States, Canada, and Europe to stay in touch and maintain Asante unity.

The road to independence was a rocky one. Asantehene Prempeh II clashed with Ghanaian national leader Kwame Nkrumah, who was Akan but of Fante background, over the control of lands originally considered part of the treasury of the Golden Stool. But when Prempeh became ill in 1960, Nkrumah helped send him to England for special medical care. The Asantehene and the prime minister of Ghana became close friends, and Kumasi soon began to rival the national capital of Accra as a center for business and education.

Asante Today

Asante pride is still very much alive in the Ashanti Region of central Ghana, the third largest of ten administrative regions in Ghana. The court of the Asantehene in Kumasi still maintains its schedule of festivals, and Asante history is evident in the traditions of goldwork and kente weaving still maintained by Asante artisans.

Women continue to play a decisive role in Asante society, especially in business and education.

The current Asantehene is Otumfuo Nana Osei Tutu II, a thoroughly modern king with college degrees in public administration and accounting from a London university. Osei Tutu II made headlines in October 2012 during an official state visit to Sweden. A box containing some of the Asante royal gold objects was snatched from his luggage in the lobby of his hotel. Several of the gold art pieces of the Asantehene's royal regalia were stolen and lost forever. The thieves were never caught, but some pieces were later recovered.

KOFI ANNAN, GLOBAL PEACEKEEPER

Few international statesmen command as much respect as Kofi Annan, who served as the Secretary-General of the United Nations between 1997 and 2006. During his term, Annan faced many serious crises, including the Rwandan genocide, the AIDS epidemic, the Kosovo crisis, the terror attacks of 9/11, and the wars in Afghanistan and Iraq. Through it all, he maintained a calm outlook, showed an ability to get all sides to the bargaining table, and gained the respect of leaders worldwide as a force for peace.

Kofi Annan was born (along with a twin sister) in Kumasi in 1938 to a Fante mother and a father who was half Asante and half Fante. Both of his grandfathers were chiefs, making him eligible to serve as either an Asante chief or a Fante chief. Upon his retirement as a businessman, Annan's father was elected governor of Asante Province. In an interview with British journalist William Shawcross, Annan said his parents influenced him: "Character was extremely important...I also learned a sense of responsibility for less fortunate people."

Annan's education led him to college in snowy Minnesota, where his friends advised him to wear earmuffs. "After I nearly froze my ears off, I realized they were right—it was an early lesson in taking local knowledge seriously," he told Shawcross. Rather than enter into Ghanaian politics, Annan became head of the UN peacekeeping force in Bosnia during the turbulent 1990s. In 2001, he and the United Nations were jointly awarded the Nobel Peace Prize for their tireless efforts to achieve world peace. Today, he continues his efforts for peace as head of the Kofi Annan Foundation.

Perhaps the most famous person of Asante descent today is Kofi Annan, who led the United Nations through a particularly difficult era on behalf of world peace.

Today, Ghana is one of Africa's most stable and prosperous nations. The Asante region is still one of the world's richest gold mining areas. Many Asante are concerned about the environmental damage caused by the latest large-scale "gold rush" occurring in the region.

The current Asantehene, Otumfuo Nana Osei Tutu II *(right)*, governs with a combination of tradition and modern political skill.

Young Asante no longer achieve their status through war. Instead, they flock to universities for better education, where their talent for trade is molded to modern business. A surprising number of ambitious Asante have become world-class sports figures, especially in professional soccer: Kumasi boasts two Ghana Premier League teams. Perhaps the most famous person of Asante descent today is Kofi Annan, the Nobel Prize–winning former Secretary-General of the United Nations.

The Asante *sumsum*, once a byword for resistance, has endured as a voice of compromise and peace. The principles of Osei Bonsu and the Golden Stool live on.

TIMELINE

c. 1500 Adanse and Akwamu, early Akan states, emerge.

c. 1680–1717 Osei Tutu establishes the Golden Stool and reigns in the Gold Coast region; Kumasi emerges as capital of the new Asante kingdom.

1717 Opoku Ware becomes Asantehene.

1742 Opoku Ware defeats Akyem, making Asante the most powerful kingdom along the Gold Coast.

1744–45 The northern peoples of Gonja and Dagomba become Asante tributary states.

1750 Opoku Ware dies; Kusi Obodu becomes Asantehene.

1764 Osei Kwadwo becomes Asantehene.

1765 Coastal states form an alliance against the Asante.

1777 Osei Kwadwo dies; Osei Kwame becomes Asantehene.

1779 Osei Bonsu becomes Asantehene.

1802 Denmark becomes the first European slaving nation to outlaw the slave trade.

1806–07 The Asante invade Fante territory but eventually retreat.

1807 Great Britain and the United States outlaw the slave trade, though not slavery itself.

1817 English expedition arrives in Kumasi to negotiate trade relations with Osei Bonsu.

1823 The Asante attack Denkyira, Wassa, Fante, and the British.

1824 Osei Bonsu, the last Asantehene to have full control of the Asante kingdom, dies.

1874 The Asante are defeated in the War of 1874; Asantehene Kofi Kakari is deposed; Mensa Bonsu is elected Asantehene.

1883 Asantehene Mensa Bonsu is deposed; anarchy follows.

1884 Kwaku Dua II becomes Asantehene; he soon dies of smallpox.

1888 Agyeman Prempeh becomes Asantehene. An Asante delegation leaves for England to protest British policy.

1896 The British occupy Kumasi; Asantehene Prempeh I and his advisers are exiled to the Seychelles Islands; the British proclaim a protectorate over Asante territory.

1900 The British demand the Golden Stool; Queen Yaa Asantewaa and the Asante chiefs declare war against the British; the Asante are defeated.

1902 Asante territory becomes the British Gold Coast Colony.

1921 Yaa Asantewaa dies.

1924 Prempeh I returns to Kumasi from exile.

1935 Prempeh II installed as Asantehene Osei Agyeman Otumfo.

1954 The National Liberation Movement (NLM) of the Gold Coast Colony is founded.

1957 The Gold Coast Colony becomes the independent nation of Ghana within the British Commonwealth.

1995 The Royal Asante Manhiya Palace opens a modern museum of Asante history.

1999 Otumfuo Nana Osei Tutu II is named Asantehene.

2012 Asantahene Tutu II visits Oslo, Norway, where several royal gold regalia objects are stolen at his hotel.

GLOSSARY

abasua Descent of a family through the mother's line.

abolition The end of something, particularly slavery and the slave trade.

Asantehene King of the Asante.

atumpan The largest "talking" drum used by Akan peoples, who consider it sacred.

civil service An administrative agency of government that is separate from the military.

colony A territory controlled or settled by an outside state.

confederacy An alliance of several states for mutual support.

coup A coup d'état; a sudden, violent overthrow of a government by a small group.

currency The form of money used in a society.

diaspora A community of people living away from their established homeland.

exile A period of forced absence from one's native land; banishment.

gyaasewahene Head of the Asante civil service.

hierarchy A system that involves ranking people according to their economic, social, or professional standing.

kente A special form of patterned cloth woven by Asante men.

Maroon An escaped slave who fought for freedom in the West Indies, Guyana, and Suriname in the seventeenth and eighteenth centuries; a descendant of such a slave.

matrilineal Relating to or determining descent through the mother's family line.

palanquin A thronelike chair supported on poles and carried by four people.

plantation A large farm for the production of a single crop, such as sugarcane, cotton, or tobacco.

protectorate The relationship of authority assumed by one power or state over a dependent one; the dependent state or territory in such a relationship.

proverb A short popular saying expressing a basic truth or wise thought.

regalia Emblems or decorations of royalty or high rank.

sahene Leader of an Asante army.

sumsum The "collective soul" of the Asante nation, embodied in the Golden Stool.

tribute Money or goods paid by a people or a state to a more powerful state.

FOR MORE INFORMATION

African Studies Association (ASA)
Rutgers University–Livingston Campus
54 Joyce Kilmer Avenue
Piscataway, NJ 08854
(848) 445-8173
Web site: http://www.africanstudies.org
Established in 1957, the ASA is devoted to enhancing the
exchange of information about Africa. It encourages the
production and dissemination of knowledge about
Africa, past and present.

African Studies Center at Boston University
232 Bay State Road
Boston, MA 02215
(617) 353-3673
Web site: http://www.bu.edu/africa
The African Studies Center at Boston University is one of
the oldest and largest research centers for African studies in the United States. A core aspect of its work is
reaching out to schools and communities to help them
learn about Africa and its diversity. Its extensive Web site
features resources for student and teachers.

Asanteman Council of North America (ACONA-USA/Canada)
P.O. Box 831883
Richardson, TX 75083
Web site: http://www.acona-usacanada.org
ACONA is the main organization representing the Asante
communities of North America, including those in
Montreal and Toronto, Canada. It provides community

support and information, as well as maintains official contact with the Asantehene in Kumasi.

Black Cultural Centre for Nova Scotia
10 Cherry Brook Road
Cherry Brook, NS B2Z 1A8
Canada
(902) 434-6223
Web site: http://www.bccns.com
This center maintains a historical and cultural archive that traces the history of black Nova Scotians. Its Web site offers information on the history of the Jamaican Maroons and escaped American slaves who settled in Nova Scotia.

Ghana High Commission in Ottawa, Canada
1 Clemow Avenue
Ottawa, ON K1S 2A9
Canada
(613) 236 0871
Web site: http://www.ghc-ca.com
The Ghana High Commission serves as Ghana's official embassy to Canada. Information regarding Ghanaians in Canada, travel to Ghana, and business information can be found through the High Commission.

Institute of African Studies
Carleton University
439 Paterson Hall
1125 Colonel By Drive
Ottawa, ON K1S 5B6

Canada
(613) 520-2600, ext. 2220
Web: http://www2.carleton.ca/africanstudies
Carleton is the only Canadian university to have a stand-
   alone institute of African studies that offers a degree
   program. The program focuses on history, modern
   African issues and culture, and the African diaspora and
   the consequences of transatlantic slavery.

Manhyia Archives
Institute of African Studies
P.O. Box AS 477
Kumasi, Ghana
(+233) 51-33971
Web site: http://www.manhyiaarchives.org
The Institute of African Studies at the University of Ghana
   established these archives as part of the Ashanti
   Research Project in 1962. It is the official archive of the
   Asantehene's Manhyia Palace in Kumasi, and it supports
   a Web site with much information.

Web Sites

Due to the changing nature of Internet links, Rosen Publishing
has developed an online list of Web sites related to the subject
of this book. This site is updated regularly. Please use this link
to access the list:

http://www.rosenlinks.com/EAC/Asant

FOR FURTHER READING

Appiah, Peggy. *Tales of an Ashanti Father*. Boston, MA: Beacon Press, 1989.

Courlander, Harold, George Herzog, and Madye Lee Chastain. *The Cow-Tail Switch and Other West African Stories*. New York, NY: Square Fish/Henry Holt, 2008.

Dubois, Laurent, and Julius Sherrard Scott. *Origins of the Black Atlantic*. New York, NY: Routledge, 2010.

Edgerton, Robert B. *The Fall of the Asante Empire: The Hundred-Year War for Africa's Gold Coast*. New York, NY: The Free Press, 1995.

Getz, Trevor R., and Liz Clarke. *Abina and the Important Men: A Graphic History*. New York, NY: Oxford University Press, 2012.

Greene, Sandra E. *West African Narratives of Slavery*. Bloomington, IN: Indiana University Press, 2011.

Konadu, Kwasi. *The Akan Diaspora in the Americas*. New York, NY: Oxford University Press, 2010.

Rees, Sian. *Sweet Water and Bitter: The Ships That Stopped the Slave Trade*. Durham, NH: University of New Hampshire Press, 2011.

Reindorf, Carl Christian. *History of the Gold Coast and Asante*. Accra, Ghana: Ghana Universities, 2007.

Ross, Doran H. *Wrapped in Pride: Ghanaian Kente and African American Identity*. Los Angeles, CA: UCLA Fowler Museum of Cultural History, 1998.

Spring, Christopher. *African Textiles Today*. Washington, DC: Smithsonian Books, in association with the British Museum Press, 2012.

Wilks, Ivor. *Forests of Gold: Essays on the Akan and the Kingdom of Asante*. Athens, OH: Ohio University Press, 1993.

INDEX

About the Author

Robert Z. Cohen was born in New York City and studied cultural anthropology with a special concentration in African studies at Boston University in Boston, Massachusetts. There, he studied several African languages, including Yoruba, Ewe, and Zulu, as well as Haitian Creole, and he has traveled around the Caribbean researching memories of African languages. Cohen moved to Budapest, Hungary, to research the language and music of the Romani (Gypsy) people. He works as a journalist and travel guide writer and leads his own klezmer band on tours around Europe and North America.

Photo Credits

Cover, pp. 18, 28, 29 Werner Forman/Universal Images Group/Getty Images; cover (background), p. 1 Triff/Shutterstock.com; p. 5 Alida Latham Danita Delimont Photography/Newscom; p. 8 Gabrel/Shutterstock.com; p. 10 Ariadne Van Zandbergen/Lonely Planet Images/Getty Images; p. 14 Marc Deville/Gamma-Rapho/Getty Images; p. 22 Max Milligan/AWL Images/Getty Images; p. 27 Jonathan C. Katzenellenbogen/Hulton Archive/Getty Images; p. 35 Universal Images Group/SuperStock; p. 37 Time & Life Pictures/Getty Images; pp. 40, 49 Universal Images Group/Getty Images; p. 44 Imago Stock & People/Newscom; p. 47 Mark Kauffman/Time & Life Pictures/Getty Images; p. 51 Jimin Lai/AFP/Getty Images; p. 52 AFP/Getty Images; back cover daulon/Shutterstock.com; cover, back cover, and interior pages graphic elements R-studio/Shutterstock.com (gold texture), brem stocker/Shutterstock.com (compass icon), Konyayeva/Shutterstock.com (banner pattern).

Designer: Michael Moy; Editor: Andrea Sclarow Paskoff; Photo Researcher: Karen Huang